KLAUS ADAMS, born 1961, train district hospital. He has worked Husemann Clinic in Buchenbach, ne 1990. He took further training in psycniatry and is a practice manager and expert in anthroposophic nursing and an IKAM auditor (International Coordination Centre for Anthroposophic Medicine at the School of Spiritual Science at the Goetheanum). He has taught for many years on healthcare and nursing training courses, is a tutor for soul exercises and other aspects of anthroposophic psychiatry, and has authored various publications on anthroposophic psychiatric nursing.

WOLFGANG RISSMANN M.D., born 1948, studied medicine in Freiburg, Germany, and Vienna, subsequently specializing in psychiatry. From 1987 to 2013 he was chief physician at the Friedrich-Husemann Clinic in Buchenbach near Freiburg. Since 2014 he has run a private practice for psychiatry in Hamburg. He works in training of medical students, physicians and other medical professionals in the field of anthroposophic medicine and psychiatry.

MARKO ROKNIC, born 1958, trained as a nurse at Herdecke district hospital. From 1990 to 2009 he was a nurse at the Friedrich-Husemann Clinic in Buchenbach near Freiburg, Germany, and since 2009 has been a nursing manager at Sonneneck Psychosomatic Clinic in Badenweiler, Germany. He took further training in psychiatric nursing and is an expert in anthroposophic nursing, a trainer in Wegman/Hauschka rhythmic massage, and a health pedagogue (AfW Freiburg). He sits on the advisory board of the association for anthroposophic nursing, and has taught for many years in healthcare and nursing training. He is a tutor for soul exercises and other aspects of anthroposophic psychiatry, and has authored various publications on health education and nursing.

FINDING INNER BALANCE

*Meditative exercises for mindfulness,
empathy and strengthening
the will*

Klaus Adams, Wolfgang Rissmann M.D.
and Marko Roknic

Translated by Matthew Barton

RUDOLF STEINER PRESS

Rudolf Steiner Press Ltd.
Hillside House, The Square
Forest Row, RH18 5ES

www.rudolfsteinerpress.com

Published in English by Rudolf Steiner Press 2020

Originally published in German under the title *Das innere Gleichgewicht finden: Seelenübungen für Achtsamkeit, Herzenskultur und Willensstärke* by GESUNDHEIT AKTIV e. V., Berlin in 2015

Picture credits: 1. J.J. Harrison; 2. Tony Hisgett; 3. Jon Sullivan; 4. Gig; 5. Chrizzles; 6. Caspar David Friedrich; 7. Arend; 8. Bernie

The rights of the authors to be identified as the authors of this work have been asserted in accordance with sections 77 and 78 of the Copyright, Designs and Patents Act, 1988

A CIP catalogue record for this book is available from the British Library

ISBN 978 1 85584 584 8

Cover by Morgan Creative
Typeset by Symbiosys Technologies, Visakhapatnam, India
Printed and bound by 4Edge Ltd., Essex

Contents

Introduction

The human being is an inexhaustible source of strength or a strength-creating process.

Novalis

The aim of this pamphlet is to offer a range of exercises that you can easily fit into your daily life to strengthen your creativity, sense of stability and inner balance. No special knowledge or ability is needed to do this. All of us have a hidden source of strength within us that we can discover and nurture.

We know that taking regular exercise — sport or walking for instance — is good for us: we become fitter, more active, and feel more fully engaged in life. This is no accident. The key idea at work here is 'practice'. Without it we don't achieve our aims whatever they may be — getting fitter, learning a musical instrument, cooking better, or succeeding at school or at work. Everything we do benefits from practice.

But what does 'practice' actually involve? Biochemist Christoph Rehm puts it like this:[1]

Practice
Practice is activity.
Practice is conscious activity.
Practice is conscious, repeated activity.
Practice means work.

Practice means: being present.
Practice means: using our will.

You can practise practising.

Activities change us.
Active practice changes us.
Learning — experiencing.
Through practice, abilities grow.

Abilities can transform themselves.
Transition.
Something ripens.
Ripe fruit no longer belong to the tree.

But practice not only benefits the body. It also strengthens the soul, and there are specific exercises for this. They have been practised for millennia all over the globe. Originally they were developed in religious contexts and as spiritual training.

In the twentieth and twenty-first centuries these practices were widely adopted again, and often recommended as a practical aid in living our lives and keeping healthy. Rudolf Steiner, who founded anthroposophy, called them 'soul exercises', describing them as a path of modern spiritual schooling, and as a source of strength in daily life.

Who are Soul Exercises Intended For?

They are for everyone who wants to cultivate their inner development in some way, rather than staying the way they are. They are helpful for all who would like to cope better with their daily lives.

Soul exercises strengthen self-confidence and concentration and help prevent us from being so easily thrown or knocked sideways by events. They are an important tool in therapeutic work during inner crises or trauma, states of exhaustion and mental illness.

Soul exercises can also be used as part of the professional coaching often necessary for complex tasks in modern employment settings and associated social challenges.

What are Soul Exercises?

They can be roughly divided into three groups:

1. Exercises for the senses;
2. Exercises for the feelings;
3. Exercises for the will.

The exercises for the senses involve sight, hearing, touch and smell. With our senses we consciously open ourselves to the world around us without too much self-involvement. By adopting a mindful stance we can refine our sense perceptions. Here we leave to one side everything we have so far learned, and attend only to the here and now. We refrain from judging or interpreting, and observe, with astonishment, how diverse and rich the world around us is. We open ourselves directly to these impressions and by doing so experience their quality in a deeper way.

Exercises for the feelings awaken our inner sense of delight, and our heartfelt response. A beautiful painting, music, and the clouds or stars at night, can give us new inner strength. Simply imagine a clear morning when the sun rises radiant over the horizon, filling the whole world with light.

Picture 1 — Observing the natural world around us in all its diversity, like the heron here in the water, is part of developing the senses.

In all such things an unshakeable sense of optimism and positivity is an enormous help. We can consciously seek out situations in daily life that affirm such feelings. We might also write them down in a personal 'Sun Journal' (see page 17) to make ourselves more aware of them.

And a third group of exercises helps us to liberate our own will and strengthen our inner resolve. We can copy out a beautiful text slowly in long-hand, making sure the motions of our hand are calm and flowing.

When walking, we can slow down and then hasten our steps again, consciously perceiving these rhythmic alternations. And we can look back on the past day in reverse, observing its events inwardly.

In such exercises we no longer feel ourselves to be externally propelled and imposed upon. We act freely, entirely from our own volition, strengthening our inner resources by performing seemingly unimportant actions with calm and patience.

Meditative Exercises for Inner Balance

The following exercises can easily be done on your own. A partner may be helpful but is not necessary.

At the end of each exercise, pay a little attention to the effect it has for you.

- Have your perceptions changed in any way?
- Are you now more attentive than you were beforehand?
- What feelings arose in you during the exercise or just afterwards?
- Do you feel your body differently?
- Do you feel refreshed or more tired?

Don't judge these feelings. It doesn't matter if you feel disappointed or irritated when something didn't work out as you expected. Simply observe what you're experiencing. If you like, record it in writing. This will enable you to look back later and see what has changed over time once you have repeated the exercise many times.

It is best to start with an exercise you feel particularly drawn to and to do it every day for a week, observing what effect it has on you. After a week you can either decide on a new exercise or continue with the first. It is important to allow a week or two for the exercise and then consciously end it — otherwise your enjoyment of it may flag.

Don't try to do too many exercises at once — just one or two is best.

1. Finding Objective Clarity

Observing an object
Find a peaceful spot at home, turn off your mobile and all other sources of noise so that you can really remain undisturbed for a quarter of an hour.

Take an ordinary domestic object — it might for instance be a cup, a pencil, a bowl, a watering can, a vase, a tool of some kind or a plate. It doesn't matter what the thing is usually used for. Now look at this object very carefully for a minute: look at it from every angle and observe every detail of it. Then describe the object as accurately as you can, but completely prosaically and neutrally, without any value judgement. Only describe what you see or feel: size (approximately), shape, colour, surface texture, weight (approximately — after you've done the exercise it can be fun to weigh it to see whether you got anywhere near the actual weight).

If you're doing the exercise on your own, you could write down what you have observed. If there are two or more of you, you could tell each other what you see.

Variations
Describe a stone, a mineral or a crystal.

What this Exercise is Good for
It strengthens your attention and therefore helps you observe your surroundings in a more detailed, differentiated, clearer and at the same time more objective way. It helps you find inner calm, gives you greater inner clarity and presence of mind.

Especially Suitable for
People who feel continually nervous, cannot easily focus, easily lose themselves in feelings, have an overactive imagination and find it hard to keep their feet on the ground.

Length of Time
Take about five or ten minutes for this exercise.

2. Finding your Inner Breathing

Drawing an object
Sit comfortably at a table, with a sheet of paper and a soft pencil. Now place an object from your daily life in front of you (cup, vase, bowl etc.) and observe it for about a minute from all angles.

Then begin to draw it. Stop repeatedly and look at the object again so that you observe it as accurately as possible. It doesn't matter whether the drawing is 'good' or not; what matters is the process of looking and reproducing.

Try also to draw the object in three dimensions and if possible to include any shadow it casts.

Finally, look calmly at the result, with no value judgement whatever. See if you succeeded in recreating the object. If not, try again next day.

What this Exercise is Good for

It enhances the effect of exercise 1 since now you not only describe the object in words but capture it in drawing, thus observing it more keenly. As you draw, continually alternate between perceiving and drawing, and thus between outer and inner. This gives rise to a kind of inner breathing, and helps you to be more patient and composed even if you may find the reverse to begin with.

Especially Suitable for

People who find it hard to focus on the task in hand and are easily distracted. Some find this exercise a great challenge since they can barely cope with doing something imperfectly. In this case it is worth not giving up too quickly but simply trying again.

Length of Time

Take five to ten minutes for this exercise.

3. Sensing the Living World

Observing a plant

For this plant observation, bring back any plant you like from a walk. Put it in a vase in front of you, and look at it calmly from all angles, with your full attention, for about five minutes.

Then describe it in words under the following headings:

- How big is it?
- What colour is it? Describe the various shades of colour. Usually a leaf, a stem or a flower will each have a wide range of different colour nuances.

- What shape is its stem? Is it angular, round, ribbed, rough or smooth?
- Are there hairs on the stem?
- Does the plant have buds or blossoms?
- Do the flowers have any fragrance?
- Can you see any fruit or seedhead?
- How many leaves can you count?
- What shape are the leaves: narrow, long or broad?
- What do you feel when you touch the leaves? Are they rough or smooth; is their edge serrated, indented or wavy?
- What is the relationship of flowers, leaves and stem to one another? Does the plant have a lot of green vegetation and small flowers, or the other way round?

Variation 1

Observe the plant in its natural location:

- What soil is it growing in? Is it clayey, stony or sandy?
- Is it growing in a meadow? In woods? By water? Between rocks? In moss?
- What do its surroundings look like? Hill, mountain, plain?
- Is the place sunny or shady, dry or damp?
- What plants and trees are growing in the vicinity?
- How big is the plant in relation to what surrounds it? Small or large?

Variation 2

At home (or at work) observe a growing plant. For instance, place two bean seeds in water for two to three days and let them swell, then plant them in a flower pot. Keep the soil moist and observe their growth each day.

What this Exercise is Good for

Stimulating the imagination, strengthening your sense of being alive, releasing you from inner rigidity. It can give you back a sense of living processes: of growth — existence — fading.

Especially Suitable for

People who feel exhausted and weak, who no longer feel trust in life and have little interest in their surroundings.

Length of Time

Take about 20 minutes for this exercise.

Picture 2 — A beautiful object for plant inspection: a poppy bud whose petals are just about to open.

4. Making Space for Creativity

Drawing a leaf

Bring back from a walk the leaf of any plant or tree, but if the latter preferably a deciduous tree. Observe all its details very carefully, feel its texture, elasticity, the structure of its blade and edge.

Now draw the leaf with a soft pencil. Start with its outlines. *But do not place the leaf on the sheet of paper and copy the outline as a template!* The drawing should be done freehand.

Try to capture the edge of the leaf with all its indentations and grooves, without losing sight of the overall shape of the leaf. Then draw the leaf-stem, the central vein of the leaf and the side veins. Your drawing should be at least as big as the leaf itself.

When you have finished, look at your drawing sympathetically and without value judgement. Try to sense what effect this exercise has had upon you. Allow it to resonate.

Variation 1

Draw the leaf in the reverse order: start with the leaf-stem and the central vein, from this allow all the finer branchings to grow outward, and only draw the edges at the end.

Some patience and inner composure is required to keep both the details and the overall shape in view. You may well find this exercise quite strenuous to begin with, requiring a good deal of concentration. You might feel impatient in your first attempts or think you're no good at drawing. If so, stop, breathe deeply ten times, and try to let go of such thoughts. It is not about doing a perfect drawing. Then try the exercise again.

At a second stage you will also find that each leaf has a certain symmetry; this is never absolute, never perfect. And this is typical for all life: every symmetry also involves some degree of asymmetry!

After a while you will notice that this exercise gives you a new kind of inner tranquillity. You gain distance from revolving thoughts and bad moods, and feel the living power that exists in leaf and plant. You will feel refreshed.

Make sure that your drawing hand does not tense up (if necessary move your fingers now and then, or shake the hand free a little).

Breathe calmly, deeply and evenly: make sure that concentration does not make you hold your breath!

What this Exercise is Good for
It helps to define yourself more clearly and gain distance from swirling thoughts. It helps rediscover wonder.

Especially Suitable for
People who easily lose themselves in outer events, who often brood and no longer find pleasure in things, who have come to regard the world with indifference.

Length of Time
Take about 15 minutes for this exercise.

Picture 3 — The fine branchings of the veins of a leaf.

5. Deep Listening

Attentive, mindful listening

Shut your eyes and listen. What do you hear? What noises, sounds, tones, moods? Which sound lasts longer and which fades immediately?

Try to differentiate the various noises, and distinguish them from each other as clearly as possible. Which are mechanical (cars, trains, buses, lorries, machines), which come from the natural world, or from household pets (dogs or cats)?

Variation 1

Attend only to natural sounds: the babbling or chattering of a brook, the sighing of a breeze, the whistling or rushing of wind, the pattering of raindrops.

If you are in the country, listen out for the sounds of nearby animals — cows, horses, sheep, goats, hens, geese, ducks.

Variation 2

Listen only to birdsong: the fluting of the blackbird, the cooing of doves, the cheep of tits, the caw of crows, the clamour of magpies, the chirrup of chaffinches.

Variation 3

Make sounds with objects around you: tap with a spoon on a wineglass, a tumbler, a bowl, a pot; ring a small bell. If you have a sounding bowl, you can also strike upon this.

Variation 4

Attend to a human voice in your vicinity, one that has nothing to do with you (this works well in the train for instance). Notice its pitch, modulation, resonance and dynamic. This enhances the exercise still further: in the tones of a voice you can also observe the mood and intention of the speaker.

Variation 5 (for groups)

You can also do the exercise in a group. All participants shut their eyes except for one, who now creates various sounds for the others. The listeners do nothing but listen and should not speak or comment. Then change over so that each person takes a turn at producing sounds.

Note: The tones should not follow each other too quickly! Silence after a tone has faded is needed to let it resonate in us fully. But don't make this too serious an affair — it should be fun.

Variation 6 (for groups)

Participants embody each sound in a gesture (without speaking). One after another they stand up and make a gesture for each tone.

Variation 7 (for groups)

Participants paint the tones and sounds in colours on paper.

What this Exercise is Good for

This exercise helps you to attend and listen very precisely again, something extremely important today in the overstimulated cacophony of our world, in which quiet, subtle tones are easily lost.

To practise such listening again seems all the more important because we are so focused nowadays on seeing, on visual stimuli. Sight is always forward- and outward-oriented whereas listening has a closer intimacy with inner experience, and encompasses also the space behind and around us.

In listening we grow as one with what we hear. This is why music generally has a uniting quality above and beyond all differences of culture and nationality. When you attend a concert with many other people, you always feel somehow connected with them all, whether it's classical music or a pop concert, whether you're in a concert hall or in the open air, and whichever part of the world you're in.

In this exercise your attention is more inwardly rather than outwardly focused. You learn also to hear subtler tones and to experience their resonance. You become aware once more of your interiority, your inner soul.

You experience both sound and silence and connect tones and noises with your feelings.

You breathe more deeply and become more centred. You feel yourself inwardly enriched and strengthened.

Especially Suitable for
People who feel isolated and lonely.

Length of Time
Take about 10 minutes for this exercise.

6. Finding Inner Breadth

Observing the skies and the weather
Go outdoors every morning or evening at a particular time, and observe the skies.

Watch the movement and shapes of clouds. First of all choose just one area of the sky and observe how the clouds are changing in colour, form, structure, density, brightness. Observe which clouds are higher and which lower in the sky, which are moving faster or more slowly. Even when the sky is thick with cloud or when it's raining you can still discern differences — the sky is never uniform, even in thick fog. On a cloudless day, observe how the tones of blue pass through different shades down to the horizon. Can you see the con-trails of aeroplanes?

Attend to heat and cold too, and to wind and moisture.

After five minutes turn away and close your eyes. Now try to recall what you have seen inwardly, and create an after-image of it. Subsequently repeat this process of observation and recreation two or three times.

Variation 1
If you have more time than usual, for instance on holiday or on a day off, do this exercise at various times of day: in the morning, noon and afternoon. Thus you can witness three different

atmospheric conditions. You will be surprised to see how the sky can change in the course of just a single day.

Variation 2 (for groups)

You can also do this exercise in a group. The group goes outdoors without speaking and each person tries to gain a first, spontaneous impression of the weather. All separately observe a portion of the sky for five minutes in silence as described above.

Next the participants turn away and allow the after-image to appear. Afterwards, in pairs, they share their observations with each other.

The whole thing is repeated two or three times, and on each occasion everyone swaps partners again.

Variation 3 (for groups)

Each member of the group tries to observe what movements the clouds are making, how they arise and disappear, and what gestures can be seen. What forces are at work here — pressure and pull, blockage and release? Next the participants turn away, close their eyes and allow what they have seen to arise in their inward eye, like a copy. Finally all can share with each other what they have experienced.

Variation 4 (for groups)

This variation leads your observation still further inward. Each member of the group again attends as carefully as possible to how the clouds form. Next, each person allows what they have observed to resonate in them, asking what mood this gives rise to within them. This requires still more mindfulness and inner stillness. When they share their experiences again about what they have experienced, it will become apparent to what degree the mood has more of an objective or subjective character.

What this Exercise is Good for

Placing yourself into the world on your own two feet, forming a counterpart to the world in which you are neither too bound up with what you see nor too distant from it. You gain an awareness that there is more to the world than human beings and matter.

You perceive the outer world more precisely. You see what inner dynamic the moving forms and structures reveal. You grasp the ongoing transformation of nature as an inner process and inner mood. This helps you become inwardly active, better define yourself vis-à-vis the world, and at the same time you find a new, more balanced relationship with it.

You can bring thinking and reality into better attunement. Your horizon opens again and grows broader.

Especially Suitable for

People who easily get stuck and find it difficult to escape from a vicious circle of some kind; people who cannot let go of things. It is also good for those who find it difficult to engage with or accompany a process of development.

Length of Time

Take about 20 minutes for this exercise.

Picture 4 — Watching the clouds in the sky — a particularly appealing exercise.

7. Discovering Positivity

Keeping a 'Sun Journal'
Get yourself a nice notebook with empty pages and on one of the first pages inscribe the title: 'My Sun Journal'.

Sit down every evening and let images of the day pass before you. In doing so, look out for an experience that especially warmed your heart or delighted you.

It might be a conversation, a picture, a flower, a landscape, the song of a bird, clouds moving across the sky, a sunrise or sunset, a tasty meal, a pleasant fragrance, a touch, a lively conversation, a lovely encounter, the sight of someone you love, a child, someone you don't know.

Write down this experience in your Sun Journal and describe it in words or paint a picture of it. You can also add a photograph, a poem, a proverb or saying, or some other text that is important to you and corresponds in some way to the experience.

Design each page as you please, in your own personal way. If you've had several lovely experiences on one day, choose the most important one for you.

After you have made your journal entry, look upon it sympathetically and get a sense for what feelings and resonances it is now eliciting in you.

Over time, you will have a whole book of positive experiences from your daily life. They will give you a vivid awareness of how rich and fulfilled your life is.

Variation
If you can't think of any positive experience and you start brooding on this, simply stop searching for one. Instead, copy out a poem that you like. In this way the daily flow of practice continues.

What this Exercise is Good for
You become aware of how many positive experiences you have each day. You learn to attend to seemingly unimportant occurrences.

You observe the world with more interest and experience more gratitude. Every day can bring a new wonder. You feel yourself strengthened.

Especially Suitable for
People who have the sense that only bad things happen to them, who feel disregarded and hurt, who are continually dissatisfied with themselves and others. In such cases there is often little energy left over to regard the world with interest.

Length of Time
Take about 10 or 15 minutes for this exercise.

8. Finding Your Calm Perspective

Looking back on the day
In the evening, sit down quietly with no external distractions, preferably shortly before you go to bed. Now review the day's experiences. Usually either the loveliest or the most irritating occurrences are first to surface. But we are not now concerned with these.

To exclude such appraisals or value judgements, go backward, step by step, through the day. Begin therefore with what you have just been doing and go back in reverse through the day's events until you get to waking up and getting up in the morning.

If you find looking back in reverse very hard to begin with, you can also first review the day from morning till evening, and then try it the other way round.

Regard everything that happened with as little emotion and value judgement as possible. When you come across experiences that trouble you or you regret, don't cling to them by thinking you should or could have done something better or different.

All you need to do is gaze upon the kaleidoscope of this past day, with all its shades and colours, as if you were in a theatre or as if you were standing on a mountain and observing these experiences from a higher standpoint. In this way you can gain more distance from them.

If your attention gets distracted at any point, simply pick up the thread again wherever you had got to.

If you have forgotten an event or occurrence, wait briefly to see if it comes back to you. If not, leave the gap in your recall as it is and move on.

It can help to write down what happened in brief note form.

Once you have finished, stop and try to feel whether the day was well-filled. Are you satisfied? Do you want to do anything different tomorrow so that you perhaps end up feeling more satisfied? But don't think too long about these things. Having completed the review, leave the day behind you.

Variation 1 (also for groups)

In meetings, difficult conversations, or conferences, it is very useful to have a review at the end, and to sum up. You can do this for yourself, on your own, or together with all the other participants.

You can have a concluding airing of views for this purpose in which each person can say what they experienced, what was good, what could be improved, and what the outcome was for them.

Variation 2

It is also good to review things at the end of a year, or at the end of a whole phase of life:

- What events were important for me?
- Where did hindrances become apparent?
- What was especially enriching and exhilarating or joyful?
- What new things did I experience?
- Which new people did I meet?
- Which occurrences and people helped me?

In this form of review, you will usually be unable to place all the events in their precise reverse sequence because they are too manifold and comprehensive.

Here it is more a matter of focusing on certain events and regarding them once more from a higher perspective.

What this Exercise is Good for

It helps you let go of the day and therefore fall asleep more easily. In our era, especially, when we are bombarded by so many events and impressions every day, and must often accomplish several tasks at once, it is good to make a conscious effort in the evening to leave behind everything we have experienced.

In daily life we usually have a forward orientation. What's coming next? What do I still have to do? What do I need to prepare for now? What is still left to do tomorrow or this week or this month?

But it is just as necessary to turn round and look back. This will help you to find your centre again, and not lose yourself too much in the outer world.

It can help you to feel calmer, and gain distance from the pressing tasks of the day; but also to gain some distance from yourself and your own concerns.

You come back to yourself more. You gain a stronger sense of your own aims, no longer driven by external necessity but from within, by you alone.

If you are severely exhausted, you will feel your life forces being renewed again.

Especially Suitable for

People who have lost their sense of direction and no longer know what is important for them, and which goals they should pursue.

It is very effective in states of severe exhaustion, poor concentration, restlessness and stress.

Length of Time

Take no more than 10 minutes for this exercise.

If you take too long, the exercise can have the opposite effect and lead you into brooding.

9. Staying Centred

Preview of the day

Set your alarm to wake up ten minutes earlier than usual — exactly the amount of time you need for this exercise, which involves a preview of the day ahead.

Start by remembering what day it is; and then:

- What am I planning to do today?
- What obligations, deadlines, and tasks must I fulfil?
- Which of these could possibly be postponed?
- What else do I want to do today?

You might like to write notes so as not to forget certain things. You can put this slip in your handbag or trouser pocket.

Or place it on your desk, stick it on your computer, your smart phone or on your daily diary.

What this Exercise is Good for

It helps you keep an overview so you don't lose yourself in what happens or in small details. It helps you actually accomplish what you have planned for the day.

It makes it easier to decide on priorities. You remain realistic and are less at risk of getting stressed.

It helps you recognize when everything is getting too much for you. You can feel better organized, and structure your day better.

Especially Suitable for

People who find it hard to organize their day.

People who feel every evening that they have achieved nothing, or that everything is too much, or that they can't bring order into their day.

People with many different social contacts, interactions or managerial responsibilities.

Length of Time

Take about 10 minutes for this exercise.

10. Preventing Forgetfulness

Being conscious where you put things
Before going to sleep in the evening, choose an object that you can put down somewhere in your surroundings — in your bedroom, bathroom, corridor, in the kitchen, sitting room or study.

It might be a picture, a photo, a pencil, a cup, a vase, a blanket, a book — it doesn't matter. All that matters is that you observe the act of placing it with wakeful attention.

Now form a clear picture of the place where you have put the object down. Consciously take this picture with you into the night.

Next morning, retrieve this picture from within you and fetch the object from its place.

A tangible example: before going to sleep, consciously pick up a file containing documents that you will need tomorrow and place it, equally consciously, where you would not normally place it. Form a vivid picture of its surroundings, as described above.

In the morning, after you get up, recall this picture. Then you will know where your file is, and you can collect it.

You can take the same object every evening and place it somewhere different each time.

What this Exercise is Good for
It improves the memory and power of recall.

Especially Suitable for
People who are very forgetful, nervous and erratic, or who find it hard to concentrate.

Length of Time
You need at most only three to five minutes for this exercise.

11. Pros and Cons: Decision-Making

Weighing up conscious decisions
Think of a decision that you have to make in the near future: a purchase, visiting relatives, an excursion, choosing a present, confirming or cancelling a particular appointment, an invitation

to the cinema, concert or meal. Don't choose an overly important or weighty decision to begin with. Once you have practised decision-making about less critical matters, then you can apply the exercise also to weightier themes.

Now take a sheet of paper and make a list of 'pros' and 'cons' related to the decision.

Put the list to one side and sleep on it. If you are still undecided the next day, give yourself two more days and then make your decision without further thought.

In the case of important life decisions, you should allow yourself a month if the situation allows it.

What this Exercise is Good for

It strengthens your decision-making powers and your capacity of judgement, and makes you less reliant on external factors. It helps you become clearer about your needs and capacities.

Nowadays we all tend to let outer factors influence us; we often act on the spur of the moment and too seldom weigh up the pros and cons. This is a skill the exercise can help us rediscover.

Especially Suitable for

People who often act spontaneously; who take their lead from others and discuss every issue with other people; who don't trust their own opinion and think others' opinions are more reliable than their own; who often do things they do not think are right merely to comply with others.

Length of Time

Take between 10 and 20 minutes for this exercise.

12. Finding Inner Stability

Practising balance

For this exercise you will need a wooden roof batten from a builders' merchant (roughly 2 cm x 5 cm and 3-5 metres long).

As preparatory exercise first calmly walk a straight line of 2 to 3 metres, fixing on a point in the room opposite your

starting point. Don't look at your feet! Walk slowly and atten-
tively. Concentrate on every step. Keep your gaze focused in this
one direction throughout.

Now place the batten on the floor and walk very close beside
it, either on the right or left, putting one foot in front of the other.
Next cross your feet: with the left foot, walk along the right side
of the batten, with the right, alongside the left.

Only after doing this, try balancing slowly on it — barefoot or in
socks or gym shoes. If the latter, they should have thin soles so that
you can feel the wood with your feet. Your arms remain relaxed
beside your body. Your back is upright, your gaze looks forward.

Make sure you do not fall off the batten. If you slip off or start
wobbling, simply place one foot on the floor, find your balance
again, and then continue.

Stay relaxed and unbothered. Don't feel you have to do it per-
fectly.

If you practise this every day, you will soon find that you gain
more self-assurance each time.

Variation 1
After the ordinary exercise, walk backwards on the batten.

Variation 2
Try closing your eyes as you balance on the batten.

What this Exercise is Good for
It gives you a better awareness of yourself and your needs, and
helps you keep your feet on the ground more surely. You gain an
experience of your equilibrium, and become more self-confident,
calm and relaxed.

Especially Suitable for
People who are very anxious and/or nervous, or stressed and
uncertain.

Length of Time
Take roughly 10 to 15 minutes for this exercise.

13. Being Self-Aware

Finding an upright stance
Stand upright, feet together. Make sure that your weight is evenly distributed on both feet. Your arms should hang down loosely by your sides. Look straight ahead.

Now slowly bend your knees, at the same time keeping your upper body and head upright like a pillar. Then raise yourself again slowly and consciously, led from within. Pause briefly, and then raise yourself on tiptoes.

If this is difficult, just lift your heels a little. Stay in that position briefly and then lower your feet to the starting position once more.

Now lean your body backward a little — until you *almost* lose your balance. Stay there for a moment and return to the upright stance.

Then lean your body forward a little until you almost fall forward. Stay there for a moment and return to the starting position again.

Next do the same in a right and then left direction.

What this Exercise is Good for

It gives you a stronger sense of self, helping you to engage better with your life and your surroundings.

You experience being consciously upright, and can inwardly strengthen this experience.

This exercise seems very simple but is very effective. Our conscious upright stance as human beings distinguishes us from other creatures. It is the sign of an I consciousness, a sense of self and self-worth.

If we are self-aware, we naturally walk upright. When we feel bad and worthless, often our shoulders slouch and our back slumps.

Especially Suitable for

People who find it hard to wake up in the morning, who feel exhausted and unsure of themselves; people who find it hard to value themselves.

Length of Time
Take about 10 to 15 minutes for this exercise.

Picture 5 — Drawn to the light, bracken fronds unfold.

14. Enhancing Your Life Forces

Practising beautiful writing
For this exercise you will need paper and if possible a fountain pen or a soft pencil, and also a text you like which gives you food for thought.

Sit comfortably at a table and copy this text slowly by hand, in cursive script but not your usual handwriting. What is important is writing carefully and precisely in a traditional long-hand script. It is like drawing each letter.

As you do this, breathe calmly and evenly. When you have finished, pause and look sympathetically at what you have written. Attend to the effect this exercise has upon you.

If you find it hard to begin with to write slowly and beautifully, this will quickly improve as you get more practice.

Variation 1
Add a curlicue to certain letters, for example to every letter E.

Variation 2
Change the slope of the letters to the left.

Variation 3
Write with your non-dominant hand (i.e. with your right hand if you are left-handed, or vice versa).

Variation 4
Write with your feet! Take a thick wax crayon or a felt pen. Make sure that the paper is pinned securely to the floor and that it is big enough to write on with your feet.

Clench the crayon or pen firmly between your big and second toes, and write out a short text in this way (one or two sentences are enough).

Your foot should move freely in the air. Don't rest on your heels! This is a way of making the feet that carry you through life more conscious and self-reliant.

What this Exercise is Good for
This is a calming exercise, that helps you concentrate better and
be more mindful. You experience the movement as a beneficial,
breathing rhythm. As you continue to practise, this markedly
enhances your life forces.

Especially Suitable for
People who are nervous and uncertain.

Length of Time
Take about 10 to 15 minutes for this exercise.

15. Finding Your Own Rhythm

Conscious walking
Walk straight ahead in as calm a tempo as you can. It doesn't
matter whether you do this indoors or outdoors. Then slowly
quicken your steps and walk as quickly as you can without
starting to run. After a while, slow down again and walk very
leisurely, until you almost come to a standstill.

Alternate a few times between these two extremes, and then
try to discover the tempo that best suits you, ignoring at present
all tasks that may await you. Focus exclusively on this walking
motion. This rhythm is *your* rhythm, and usually coincides with
the tempo of your heartbeat.

If you walk faster than your individual tempo, you quickly
become breathless, tense and soon feel tired. If you walk more
slowly than is natural for you, you easily start feeling sluggish
and dreamy. In both cases you lose the connection to yourself
and your surroundings.

In the medium rhythm that belongs to you, you perceive both
yourself and the world around you. Then, even when walking for longer periods, you will hardly tire but will feel refreshed and enlivened.

This exercise is very ancient and was cultivated back in the
time of Babylon. The following poem dates back to that era:[2]

> Behold the man who walks there:
> Not like an old man and not like a child;

Walking in health and not in sickness,
He does not walk too quickly
Nor too slowly.
Behold him, and you will see how the sun
Measures the span of the heavens.

Nowadays this wholesome kind of walking has been rediscovered as 'meditative walking'. Experienced walkers will also be aware of their own individual walking rhythm, neither too fast nor too slow. With it, they can walk for hours without tiring.

Variation
Walking in your ideal rhythm, clap your hands at each step.

What this Exercise is Good for

It helps you to focus on the movement of your own body. You can experience the alternation between stress and sluggishness, and thus find your centre, your individual balance. In this way you can shrug off both stress and anxiety.

Especially Suitable for

People who are nervous and anxious.

Length of Time

Take about 30 minutes for this exercise. You can also practise it while walking or hiking.

16. Finding Your Place of Inner Calm

Practising juggling
For this exercise you will need three juggling balls or tennis balls.

Even if you have never juggled before, or are daunted by the skill of professional jugglers at the circus, just have fun with this exercise and enjoy its playful ease.

First relax by swinging your arms backward and forward and shaking your legs out a little.

Then stand upright and take care that you are well-balanced on your feet. Your weight should not shift too much either to the balls of your feet or your toes.

Now lean as far forward as you can, then slowly regain the vertical position vertebra by vertebra. Next start with a small preparatory exercise:

Pick up one of the balls in your right hand and pass it in a small curve from above to the left hand, which receives it like a bowl. Now the left hand passes the ball back to the right hand in the same way.

Continuing with these giving and receiving gestures, the curves described by the balls in each hand can grow larger each time so that the movement flows and the form becomes that of a horizontal figure of eight whose midpoint lies in front of the middle of your body.

Now the actual exercise starts:

1. Throw a ball up with one hand and catch it with the same hand. Your palm is facing upward and your arm is bent at the elbow. Then it's the turn of the other hand.
2. Throw a ball up with one hand and catch it with the other, then continue in alternation.
3. Now take two balls and throw the first diagonally upward with one hand. As its reaches the highest point of its curve and is falling back again, throw the second ball upward with the other hand in the opposite, diagonal direction. Catch the balls one after the other.

   Then change the sequence to the other way round.
4. Now take the third ball as well and bravely juggle with all three at once. Practice makes perfect!

It does not matter in the least if the balls fall on the ground. You can also intentionally let them fall. Letting go is as much a quality of juggling as catching.

Make sure you stay upright and look straight ahead, not at the floor or the ceiling. Don't hold your breath either, otherwise you'll get tense. Don't get too ambitiously fixated on success. The exercise is meant to be playful and fun.

What this Exercise is Good for

You engage in a pleasurable activity and remain relaxed and focused.

You can let go of thoughts and feelings, which are not important right now!

This helps you to find inner calm and both inner and outer equilibrium.

Especially Suitable for

People who are stuck in their head, and find it hard to let go of thoughts. People who are caught up in the hamster wheel of daily life.

Length of Time

Take about 10 to 15 minutes for this exercise.

17. Looking with New Eyes

Observing a picture

In this group exercise you look together at a picture, preferably an art print or a painting. Experience has shown that the works of both old masters and more recent artists are suitable for this: the latter might include paintings by Caspar David Friedrich, Paul Cézanne, Franz Marc, Vincent van Gogh, Pablo Picasso or Mark Rothko.

Participants should gather round the painting so that they can all see it well. Look at the image for about two to three minutes in silence. Then it is covered up or turned to face the wall.

Now each participant should try to recreate the picture inwardly; and then describe what they have seen: colours, shapes, objects, landscape.

It is simply a matter of describing what you have seen.

You should not interpret or evaluate the painting.

You can also look at the painting repeatedly, and only then describe your impressions of it.

Picture 6 — An artwork well suited for observation: The 'Chalk Cliffs at Ruegen' by Caspar David Friedrich.

In a second stage, the participants look at the painting again and say how it affects them. What do you feel while looking at it? What feelings does it elicit in you? It is now no longer a matter of describing something objectively but you can also convey all your subjective impressions of it.

In a third stage the painting is observed with particular questions in mind: What is this painting trying to tell me? What may the painter's intentions have been? What title would I give this painting? Here we are trying to encompass the totality of the painting and its expressive qualities.

Variations

Do the picture observation in the evening. Next morning the participants say what they remember and how the painting affected them during the night (did anyone dream about it?)

Each person should focus on what particularly strikes them in their memory of it, what mood it has left, and what the painting says to them.

What this Exercise is Good for

It deepens observation, and the experience of feelings evoked by colours and forms. It helps you to become aware of an inward response without the need to interpret it, to develop new sensitivity, and to free yourself from subjective thoughts and feelings that are hampering you. It teaches you to look with new eyes, to strengthen your memory and to develop a focus on what is important amongst a mass of details.

Especially Suitable for

People who tend to superficiality and feel the world to be of little significance, who regard their surroundings with indifference and find it hard to open up to others.

Length of Time

Take about 30 minutes for this exercise.

18. Inward Refreshment

Conscious smelling

This exercise is best done in groups.

You will need 10 small bottles containing different smells and fragrances. Best are etheric oils or spices. Remove any labels and just number the bottles. Make a list in which you note which bottle contains which smell or fragrance.

In the group, pass round five of the bottles at a time and let the participants smell each one.

It is better to subdivide larger groups otherwise it can get too chaotic.

The aim of the game is to tell which smell each one is. Participants write down what they think, and afterwards can discuss the results together.

Variation 1

Do the exercise in pairs. Each person describes the qualities of each smell to the other, and says what they think it is. It is good to say things like 'It smells like...' Also see if you can connect any memories with the smell.

Variation 2 (on your own)

The next time you go for a walk, try to smell everything you encounter: tree bark, blossoms, grasses, leaves, earth, stones, sand.

Or else rub different herbs between your fingers and smell them.

What this Exercise is Good for

You focus your attention on smells and the feelings associated with them.

Smells have a direct connection with feelings and can be assigned straightaway to 'pleasant fragrances' or 'unpleasant smells'. These associations are completely involuntary and immediate. By focusing on smell in this way, a new interest in the world awakens, and in all the associations thus evoked. You can feel enlivened, refreshed and fortified.

Especially Suitable for

People who are exhausted and apathetic, and have no interest in their surroundings.

Length of Time

Take about 20 to 30 minutes for this exercise, depending on how big the group is, and how many smell samples you want to provide.

19. Wellbeing and Discernment

Tactile experiences

This exercise works best with two people.

You will need an object that can be touched with closed eyes. Natural materials are best suited for this: tree bark, wood; smooth, rough, round or angular stone; animal pelt or fur; tree fruits (chestnuts, beech nuts, acorns).

Sit down with your partner and close your eyes. Your partner gives you an object that you touch and feel silently for about a minute. Then describe what you felt with your hands.

The aim of the exercise is not to guess what the object is but to describe carefully and accurately what you feel: the shape, size, weight, surface texture, temperature etc. of the object. Here it also helps to consider its spatial orientation in terms of right/left, front/back, top/bottom.

Then swap roles and repeat the exercise.

Instead of closing your eyes, you can also feel the object under a cloth.

Variation 1

Do the exercise in a larger group, in pairs. At the end all the participants describe their experiences to the rest of the group.

Variation 2

Place the objects in various boxes or containers and cover these with a cloth so that they can't be seen. Have participants feel in each box without looking.

Variation 3

Use your feet to feel the objects instead of your hands. To do this you could set up a 'course' composed of various materials (sand, earth, stone, water, mud, gravel, moss, pine needles etc.) over which participants are led barefoot and 'blind'.

Picture 7 and 8 — Tactile contrasts: the spiny shells of chestnuts and the delicate fleece of willow catkins.

What this Exercise is Good for

Calming down, finding a sure centre. Being fully present in your hands (or, in variation 3, in your feet).

This activity creates a sense of wellbeing, of soothing stimulus; of being alert and active without getting nervous.

Developing composure and calm in movement (variation 3). Feeling centred.

Giving 'nourishment' in equal measure to both the mind and the feelings. As you look for the right words to describe the experiences, you can remain fully present with yourself and your own experiences, in inward, engaged activity.

Especially Suitable for

People who are nervous and restless, or sluggish and uninterested; people who are caught up in their own thoughts and feelings and cannot get free of them.

Length of Time

Take about 10 minutes for each object.

20. Conversations Without Words

Communicating with rods

This exercise is for two partners together. You will need non-slip shoes and two rods or sticks about a metre long, for instance sawn-off broom handles rounded at both ends or copper rods provided with protective caps at both ends.

First acquaint yourself with your rod: touch it (also with eyes closed). Roll it the length of your body. Place it on your head, balance it on your palms, on the back of your hands. Let it fall to the ground, and perceive its resonance and sound quality.

Now stand upright opposite your partner, both of you inclined slightly toward each other. Bend your knees a little, and your back can be a little rounded.

Now hold your rod at each end with the middle of your palms, without grasping it. The palms only have as much contact with the rod as is needed to stop it falling. Each partner holds their rod parallel to the other's rod and in contact with it.

Try out various strengths of push and counter-push to gain a sense of the quality of this meeting.

Now hold the rods at different heights: with arms hanging down (thus at hip level), with bent arms (at chest height), with upstretched arms (above the head). Alternate between these levels now and then, and feel the different qualities that arise.

Now carefully let the rods swing back and forth, and in this way begin to have a silent 'conversation' with your partner. In doing so you can 'question' and 'answer', 'act', 'listen' and 'react'. Try to use as little strength as possible. The whole thing should remain a playful dialogue.

Caution: Don't move abruptly or forcefully as you could hurt your partner. Make sure the rods don't slip off or 'drill' into your partner's body.

Variation
While doing this exercise, also move around in the room.

What this Exercise is Good for
You develop an awareness of your body and its reactions and responses. You feel your muscles. You learn to define yourself but also to engage with the other. You develop a healthy balance between attentiveness to others and self-assertion.

Especially Suitable for
People who tend to adapt to others, and who find it hard to perceive or properly attend to their own wishes and needs.

Length of Time
Take about 10 to 15 minutes for this exercise.

Soul Exercises — The History and Background

*Meditation teaches us to experience life from within outwards.
However important the external aspects of life may be, behind
the easily available surface of things is concealed an equally
important yet largely silent portion of reality.*

Arthur Zajonc[3]

Meditative exercises originate in ancient spiritual traditions. We find them in pre-Christian times in many religions, primarily in Asia. In Hinduism and Buddhism lives a certainty that human beings participate in a cosmic and supersensible world. The gods are felt to indwell both nature and humankind.

Meditation is regarded as a way of gaining spiritual experiences, and communicating with the divine realm. The preconditions for such practice include inner stillness, turning away from the outer world, mystic contemplation, reverence for higher truths and harmonious inner life.

Meditation is done using images and words (mantras) but also movements (e.g. the Asanas in yoga) as well as conscious schooling of the breath. Mindfulness meditation, which has gained currency today, has its roots in these traditions.

A second era began with Christianity. In medieval times, especially, a culture of the heart began which we still find today in Christian monasteries, and orders of monks and nuns. In these orders, strict rules govern the alternation between prayer and practical work ('ora et labora').

Additionally, asceticism and abstinence often formed part of such practices. People cultivated an intense religious feeling life, which found its expression in religious painting, sculpture in cathedrals, liturgical music, and special performances at Christmas and Easter. Christian mysticism is part of this context.

Well-known figures in this tradition are Meister Eckhart, Johannes Tauler, Hildegard of Bingen and others.

A new era began with the twentieth century. Science and materialism had radically changed people's outlook on life, replacing spiritual and religious experience with a kind of sober pragmatism. Only what people perceived through their ordinary senses and powers of reason was regarded as valid.

Technology and industrialization led to a dissolution of traditional societal connections and ties, and engendered a feeling about life founded primarily on utilitarian values. Material gain and prosperity became the exclusive focus of many people's lives.

But hand in hand with this came a new longing for spiritual values and meditative experience.

Responding to these needs, the philosopher and spiritual scientist Rudolf Steiner (1861-1925), with his followers and colleagues, developed anthroposophy as a path of spiritual knowledge and schooling for modern people.

This starts from the needs and plight of modern human beings and seeks to create a more human-scale civilization, helping us to see daily life in a greater spiritual context once more and thus make our culture more humane.

Anthroposophic Meditation

The spiritual path of anthroposophy includes a great number of meditative exercises, which Steiner termed 'soul exercises'. These address all faculties and capacities of the soul, extending and strengthening our sense perceptions, thinking, feeling life and will. Their point of departure is in both eastern and western methods and in Christianity, but they offer a new emphasis that takes full account of our lives in the modern world.

Anthroposophic meditation is not based on yoga-type body positions or training of breathing but starts directly from our mental and emotional experience. This does however encompass the body too in healthy, secondary fashion: our breathing deepens, the body grows warm, life forces are stimulated.

Anthroposophic meditation initially involves sensory exercises: sight, hearing, smell, touch, the perception of balance and movement. Attention is focused on particular details to give rise to a picture that is as accurate as possible. Then one pauses and attends with complete openness to the echo or resonance in us of these observations. Thus we can achieve a rhythmic alternation between attentive focus and open awareness — like an inner breathing.

A further emphasis of anthroposophic meditation is on will exercises, above all ones known as 'review' exercises. For example, we can recall each day's events in reverse sequence (see page 18). This requires alert attention and effort. By doing this we enhance our memory and stimulate the will.

Another form of review is to look back on life at the end of a year or when embarking on a new phase. Here we don't just focus on ourselves but on our whole social milieu and our destiny connections with others. This enlarges our horizon and creates a healthy distance from ourselves.

Then there is the review of particular events or phenomena. For instance, we can speak poems backward, line by line, or picture plays in reverse, scene by scene.

In all review exercises we encounter ourselves and strengthen our will in a healthy way. Thus anthroposophic meditation unites two aspects: in sensory exercises we open ourselves selflessly to the world; in will exercises we strengthen our personality and character.

Soul Exercises and Personal Health

> *But every power that flows from the source of spiritual life is something that we can configure into art…Why therefore should we not be able to engender health, since this is the epitome of life?*
> Ernst von Feuchtersleben[4]

The idea of nurturing personal health can likewise be found in pre-Christian times and ancient religions. Spiritual work and practice also had the aim of strengthening the health of both body and soul. This idea culminated in pre-Christian approaches to medicine and healing.

Hippocrates (460-370 BC), who lived in ancient Greece, is regarded as the father of scientific medicine. In Hippocratic writings we find a prime focus on prevention. The Hippocratic physician tries to form a comprehensive picture of a patient: he gives them a physical examination, and asks them questions about their biography, way of life, profession, character but also the environment in which they live, their home, the atmospheric conditions prevailing there. He considers the effect of the changing seasons, asks them about drinking water, climate, diet and exercise habits. Thus the doctor focuses not only on an illness or a condition but above all on everything that may nurture and promote health.

Accordingly, the first measure the doctor will often propose is a change in lifestyle. Only after this do medicines and medical interventions follow.

This involves a kind of 'art of life' which encompasses six fields:

1. Light and air
2. Food and drink
3. Work and rest
4. Sleep and waking
5. Excretion and elimination
6. Stimulation of the feelings and inner equilibrium

Hippocratic medicine remained an influence on medical practice until well into the nineteenth century.

At the beginning of the twentieth century, the life reform movement took up the idea of preventive healthcare in its own fashion. Initiatives arose such as the youth movement (e.g. the Scouts and Guides, and the Wandervogel in Germany), choral societies, whole food diets, progressive education, allotments, abstinence from alcohol, naturism and naturopathy.[5]

Since then people's way of life has continued to change dramatically, with environmental degradation, the automation and mechanization of work, the industrialization of food production and dietary impoverishment. An existential crisis arose, partly due to the decline of the family as a traditional force of social coherence, and to increasing anonymity of city life. This led to a widespread inner sense of weariness in people, often coupled with loss of meaning and motivation.

We have lost a natural harmony between ourselves and nature, and social harmony between each other. For decades now, this has led to an increasing interest in ideas of preventive health.

One of the concepts developed in consequence is that of salutogenesis (Latin *salus* = salvation, wholeness, wellbeing, health; and Greek *genesis* = origin), developed by the Israeli medical sociologist Aaron Antonovsky (1923-1994). He formulated the term 'sense of coherence' to describe our ability to respond flexibly to stress and upset:[6]

The sense of coherence is a global orientation expressing the degree to which we possess a pervasive, lasting and yet dynamic feeling of trust that:

1. the stimuli appearing in life within our inner and outer surroundings are structured, predictable and explicable;
2. we possess the resources to meet the demands that these stimuli make upon us;
3. these demands are challenges which are rewarded by our exertions and committed response.

This salutogenesis orientation is diametrically opposed to the pathogenesis model.

Pathogenesis focuses on illness, on deficiencies and pathogens (viruses, bacteria) or inner trauma. Salutogenesis attends to what makes us healthy and sustains us, to what we possess rather than what we lack; to the resources we have and how to strengthen them.

Salutogenesis and Anthroposophy

From the beginning, Rudolf Steiner developed anthroposophy with a salutogenesis approach. The concern with spiritual ideas aims not only to broaden our personal horizon but also to promote our health.

For health and inner equilibrium, Steiner describes the following six basic exercises:

- Learning to think clearly and objectively: for at least five minutes each day, elaborate specific, relevant thoughts about an external and very ordinary object. What is it made or composed of? How was it made and where does it come from? What can it be used for?
- Control of the will: each day undertaking a simple, insignificant, self-chosen action, one you decide upon intentionally; it must not arise from your own needs or desires, nor be something required of you externally.
- Becoming more composed and steady in your feelings: feel your feelings deeply but do not allow them to lead to uncontrolled emotional reactions and actions.
- See the world positively: in all daily experiences, seek the positive, though without surrendering your critical faculty. Do not suppress your power of judgement but actively look for the positive aspects of everything.
- Being open and receptive for new experiences: do not hamper your encounter with the world through preconceptions; be open to new things, events and ideas, unprejudiced.
- Practise the five exercises above in alternation, creating an inner harmony between them and redressing any one-sided aspects you discover in yourself.

These six exercises are intended to school the psyche. At the same time they help to shape our daily life in positive ways.

Soul Exercises in Psychotherapy

The targeted use of meditative exercises in psychotherapy only began in the early twentieth century.

In the field of psychiatry, Italian psychiatrist and psychotherapist Roberto Assagioli (1888-1974) was one of the first to integrate elements of Hindu and Buddhist meditation, and Christian mysticism, into his psychotherapeutic work.

In his 'psychosynthesis' he added specific inner practices to the form of psychoanalysis current at the time, which was based on the work of Sigmund Freud and Carl Gustav Jung. Assagioli starts from mindfulness exercises (e.g. self-identification and de-identification, imagination and visualization techniques, auditory evocation and other sense perceptions) and primarily develops will exercises.[7,8]

Karlfried Count Dürckheim (1896-1988) is one of the pioneers of spiritual psychotherapy. He lived for many years in Japan in order to learn about Zen Buddhism. The 'Initiatic Therapy' founded by him and Maria Hippius, which includes body therapy elements alongside elements of Zen Buddhism, as well as art and drama, links up with Alfred Adler's Individual Psychology and Carl Gustav Jung's Depth Psychology.[9]

Since the 1970s, the concept of 'mindfulness' developed by Jon Kabat-Zinn (born 1944) has become well-known throughout the world.[10] This unites elements of Hatha yoga, Vipassana and Zen Buddhism, and is used in the programme of Mindfulness-Based Stress Reduction (MBSR) for groups. In 1979 Kabat-Zinn founded the Stress Reduction Clinic in Massachusetts, USA, treating people suffering from exhaustion and life crises. The MBSR starts by teaching people not to apply value judgements but to remain patient, open and trusting: to accept what is, perceive what's happening each moment, let go of fixed ideas, and experience the present moment instead of staying stuck in the past or living for the future.

Bodywork is added to this: diaphragm breathing and particular (yoga) body positions, body-scan, walking meditations and the integration of mindfulness into daily life.

The successes of the MBSR programme are so striking that since the 1990s the principle of mindfulness has found its way into the most varied form of modern psychotherapy. The best-known of these is Marsha Linehan's Dialectical-Behavioural Therapy.[11]

Soul Exercises in Anthroposophic Medicine

A new outlook is needed because we find ourselves today in a
fundamentally new situation, and we can only understand ourselves
if we know that we are also beings of spirit.

Wolf-Ulrich Klünker[12]

Soul exercises are an integral part of anthroposophic medicine and a primary focus of anthroposophic psychotherapy. They are indicated not only for emotional and mental problems and crises but also for bodily illnesses, and this is because sustaining a course of treatment also depends upon patients themselves taking responsibility for their condition and working to cure it.

Illness is more than a deficiency; it is always also a challenge to us to participate in the process of healing. Soul exercises enable patients to cope better with their illness, to develop new interest in the world and to rediscover their own power of initiative.

Use of soul exercises in a therapy setting requires prior training in a therapeutic profession. Diagnostic and therapeutic training is needed to guide patients in their use of the exercises. Especially in psychiatry and in psychosomatic medicine, adequate knowledge of clinical pictures is necessary to be able to assess the value and action of each exercise. Only then can a therapist prescribe exercises tailored to the individual.

In addition, it is important for therapists themselves to practise the exercises. It is not enough simply to give a patient an exercise. Only our own experience with it allows us to teach another how to do it.

For many years now, nurses at the Friedrich-Husemann Clinic in Buchenbach near Freiburg, Germany, have been systematically trained in these exercises. These courses are also open to other participants from outside the clinic, and are recognized by the Medical Section at the Goetheanum.

Single and Group Therapy

All exercises in this booklet are described to show each person how to use them on their own. However, in the case of mental illness, this is not always feasible.

It has therefore proven helpful to give regular therapeutic guidance to patients using them, supporting them in targeted use of the exercises. Thus patients can have the necessary personal and therapeutic support.

The aim of such therapeutic situations is always only to support patients until they can practise the exercises on their own, unaided.

Some exercises are more useful in a group context. This applies chiefly to the picture observation exercise (p. 31), the listening exercise (p. 12), the smelling exercise (p. 33) and observation of the sky and the weather (p. 14).

The exercises with writing and drawing can also be done and taught in a group. This makes dialogue possible between the participants, and encourages individuals to undertake this work on their own too.

Acknowledgements

Thanks to all who helped to develop these exercises, chiefly patients at the Friedrich-Husemann Clinic. In many years of therapeutic work with them, they showed us how the exercises can help people in different crises and states of mental illness.

Thanks to those who took part in courses on burnout prevention. They taught us which approaches are most effective in states of exhaustion and life crisis.

Thanks to our colleagues at the Friedrich-Husemann Clinic — nurses, physicians, psychologists and therapists; and also at Herdecke district hospital (Germany), Arlesheim Clinic (Switzerland) and the Bernard Lievegoed Clinic (Holland), for many years of dialogue and discussion about the soul exercises.

We are also very grateful for the training courses run over many years by Ilse Müller and Rudy Vandercruysse.

Thanks to the former manager of the Friedrich-Husemann Clinic, Silvia Renkewitz, for her interest and her financial support of the booklet.

Thanks to Gudrun Adams, Silke Michaels, Annerose Nisser, Tina Posselt, Helena Rissman and Petra Roknic, who helped with the style and content of the booklet.

We would like to give special thanks to the journalist Anette Bopp, who oversaw editing of the booklet and ensured the language used in it was clear and comprehensible. We thank Dr Stefan Schmidt-Troschke and the GESUNDHEIT AKTIV association for anthroposophic medicine for making publication of the booklet possible in its present form.

Notes

1. Rehm, Christoph, *Jonglieren, ein Übungsweg*, Verlag Urachhaus, Stuttgart 1986.
2. See: Steiner, Rudolf, GA 126, lecture of 30.12.1910.
3. Zajonc, Arthur, 'Das Innere pflegen', in: *a tempo*, August 2014, Verlag Freies Geistesleben and Urachhaus, Stuttgart.
4. Feuchtersleben, Ernst von, *Zur Diätetik der Seele*, ed. Renate Riemeck, Verlag Urachhaus, Stuttgart 1980, p. 61.
5. Huppertz, Michael, *Achtsamkeitsübungen. Experimente mit einem anderen Lebensgefühl*, Junfermann Verlag, Paderborn 2013.
6. Antonovsky, Aaron, *Salutogenese. Zur Entmystifizierung der Gesundheit*, dgvt-Verlag, Tübingen 1997, p. 36.
7. Assagioli, Roberto, *Psychosynthesis: A Manual of Principles and Techniques*, Thorsons 1999.
8. Assagioli, Roberto, *The Act of Will*, Synthesis Center Inc., 2010.
9. Dürckheim, Karlfried von, *Erlebnis und Wandlung. Grundlagen der Selbstfindung*, Suhrkamp Verlag, Frankfurt am Main 1993.
10. Kabat-Zinn, Jon, *Mindfulness Meditation in Everyday Life & Exercises and Meditations*, BetterListen, CD audio 2014.
11. Bohus, Martin and Berger, Matthias, 'Die Dialektische-Behaviorale Psychotherapie nach Marsha Linehan. Ein neues Konzept zur Behandlung von Borderline-Persönlichkeitsstörungen', *Nervenarzt* 1996 (67), 911-923.
12. Wolf-Ulrich Klünker, 'Eine Neubesinnung ist nötig', in: *Flensburger Hefte, Aspekte anthroposophischer Psychotherapie*, Issue 82, autumn 2003, p. 125.

Further Reading

Enlivening the Chakra of the Heart, Florin Lowndes
Knowledge of the Higher Worlds, How is it Achieved?, Rudolf Steiner
Raising the Soul, Warren Lee Cohen
Understand Your Temperament!, Dr Gilbert Childs
What is Anthroposophic Medicine?, Michaela Glöckler

Relevant anthologies by Rudolf Steiner:
Heart Thinking (Ed. M. Maria Sam)
Imagination (Ed. E. de Boer)
Intuition (Ed. E. de Boer)
Mindfulness and Reverence (Ed. A. Neider)
The Rose Cross Meditation (Ed. C. Haid)
Self-Knowledge (Ed. A. Neider)
Six Steps in Self-Development (Ed. A. Baydur)
Strengthening the Will (Ed. M. Maria Sam)